RIFFRAFF

LOUISIANA STATE UNIVERSITY PRESS }|{ BATON ROUGE

POEMS

STEPHEN CUSHMAN

RIFFRAFF

Published by Louisiana State University Press
Manufactured in the United States of America
LSU Press Paperback Original
First printing

DESIGNER: *Mandy McDonald Scallan*
TYPEFACE: *Whitman*
PRINTER: *IBT Global*

Library of Congress Cataloging-in-Publication Data

Cushman, Stephen, 1956–
 Riffraff : poems / Stephen Cushman.
  p. cm.
 ISBN 978-0-8071-3760-4 (pbk. : alk. paper)
 I. Title.
 PS3553.U745R54 2011
 811'.54—dc22

                                                              2010024631

The paper in this book meets the guidelines for permanence and durability of the Committee on Production Guidelines for Book Longevity of the Council on Library Resources. ∞

Acknowledgments: *Archipelago:* "Presbyopia"; *American Scholar:* "Politics"; "Under the Auspices"; *Backwards City Review:* "Taste the Fresh Juice of the Pomegranates"; *Chatauqua Literary Journal:* "Old Dogs"; *Drunken Boat:* "Pair of Anklets, Mughal, India, Seventeenth Century," "Sacrificial," and "Wind Advisory"; *Hedgehog Review:* "Jogger at the Bloody Angle" and "To Future People"; *Hollins Critic:* "Blurbs for Thursday;" *International Literary Quarterly:* "American Dream" and "Aramaic in Sednaya"; *ISLE:* "Coastal Acoustics"and "Hydrological"; *Jestschrift for Jerome McGann:* "A Way with Words"; *Literary London:* "Lower Window for Ventilation"; *Mickle Street Review:* "Sherman, After Louisiana"; *Ploughshares:* "Ten Tankas"; *Prague Revue:* "After the Bombings"; *The Recorder:* "General Post Office, Dublin"; *Smartish Pace:* "Cabin Fever," "Love Junk," "Patriotic," and "Striking Distance"; *Southwest Review:* "Home on Leave"and "Smaller Dog"; *Streetlight:* "Cross Country Practice" and "Windshake"; *Virginia Quarterly Review:* "Beside the Point"; *Yale Review:* "Missionary Position" and "Ways People Wake."

Grateful acknowledgment is made for funding from the Dean of the College of Arts and Sciences and the Vice President for Research and Graduate Studies, University of Virginia.

CONTENTS

RIFFRAFF

DARK MEAT

Would that I could
in everything give thanks,

wishy-washy overcast
and succoring sun alike,

in inmates' eyes that miss the sky
something awful, something fierce,

just as much as in chance earshot
of a hawk that scrapes said sky with its cry;

would that it were so easy to find
the sacred in the massacred,

that no *oh dear, alas, alack*
here be heard.

HYDROLOGICAL

Three quick inches drenching the ridge
make a textbook day to study drainage,
every cleft a creek and every creek
a moiling seethe, dangerous to wade
when the watershed funnels its dousing this way,
brand new flumes where nothing ran before,
outcrops and ledges spewing like gargoyles,
and a thousand white veins,
braiding down, branching backwards,
mapped against the mountainside
as clearly as dye, shot through a heart,
traces the flow that ravels and ramifies.

FROM A VISITOR'S GUIDE

Here on the island's east side,
where cliffs white with guano shear to the sea,
slick moss, invisible, grows on the rocks
wet by the surf, staining them black.
Many who venture onto these rocks
have slipped and fallen into the sea.
Tides and the undertow make rescue unlikely.
During and after a storm, or even in calm
when a storm is blowing miles offshore,
huge waves called combers come without warning
and sweep away anything caught in their path.
When watching the surf, maintain a bulwark
between you and the view.

UNDER THE TABLE

Two spruce islands wrapped in rocks
square off across a skinny strait,
but the moon tugs, tide turns,
and connection's arcing bar
of sand and gravel, shells and stones,
rises in a ridge between them.

CARDINAL RULE

Red feathers, orange beak, black mask,
why keep attacking the glass
of my window? Of all the idiocies,
mistaking your beauty
for that of a rival you're eager to mutilate
beats anything. I've known a few haters
and a few more self-lovers.
But this twisted version
and in one so ravishing?

UNDER THE AUSPICES

Five common crows harassing a hawk,
broad-winged red-tail coasting updrafts
above a field of cedar cut
and piled high for winter burning,

drive him to evasive action,
sudden nose-dives, steep chandelles,
loop the loops to lose a lunch,
as he, with every bank and roll,

diagrams a dogfight move,
and who knows what could be at stake here,
hunting rights or nest protection,
unless it's just a matter of fun,

what corvidae do on a blue afternoon,
no harm meant, as the first two tire
and peel off, then two more, until there's one
alone on his tail, a chunky black suffix

in the daredevil grammar of classical sky.

PRICKLY BRAMBLES

Blackberry bushes clumped in thickets
on dirt-road shoulders, in drainage ditches,
along the banks of dried-up creek beds,
bust right out with small white flowers

and I'm a walking thunderstorm,
hooks in the eyes, thorns in the throat,
head a downpour, and all my tissues
hysterical with histamines, enough,

you'd think, to overcome reluctance
to take anything that could impede
bulldozer driving or, worse,
increase excitability, especially

in children or in those, I guess,
still wired like them and maybe better off
for never having smelled May's breath
or seen two mockingbirds into their mating

all the way through, she hopping left,
as does he, she hopping right, as does he,
then the airborne bedlam of chevrons

gone in a blinding clap of sneeze.

STRIKING DISTANCE

And you thought it safe to walk in the woods
miles from muggings, head-on collisions, suicide bombers,
when all of a sudden, within easy reach
of juicy calf or bony knee, the buzzing breaks out,
a sound of loose pieces vibrating fast
at the end of a tail lifted in anger,
music to face one average afternoon,
when risk felt distant and the odds
of fang and coil on a well-traveled trail
infinitesimal.
            Freeze and show it
there's nothing to fear? Bolt and hope
to outrun the lunge? Or turn and see
the sycamore sapling rattling its last
desiccated leaf in a venomous breeze.

CABIN FEVER

Whoever called them crow's feet
fussed too much before a mirror
and couldn't be bothered to see
big black birds strut so glossy
across new snow, fresh and dense,
putting one foot in front of the other
like the mourning dove, who waddles,
though not like the jay, the junco,
the white-throated sparrow, each of whom hops,
feet together, always landing
side by side.
        After two days
their prints in moonlight score the snow
with quotation marks, hundreds of sets
of captain's bars, or runic z
doubled in pairs again and again
in stuttered inscription, an ancient charm
for winter night, which scarifies,
with equals signs, the corners of our eyes.

FOUL-WEATHER FRIENDS

Who needs those
who high-tail home
the moment things cool?

Better the ones
who flock in thick
as soon as it's icy,

much as the feeder
vacant in thaw
smarts just a bit.

WINTER TACTICS

I aim to sit
here all day
facing south
while the sun
outflanks and
enfilades me
with its fire.

EARPLUGS

With what I make, our house must stay
too small for peace and quiet,
but even I can afford to pay
for plugs that pacify it.

One soft wad of silicone
pressed flat across each ear,
and just like that I'm all alone
with wife and children near.

Howling dogs or heavy metal
thundered from a speaker
have always managed to unsettle
this compulsive seeker

after silence. But not anymore.
Now I'm deaf as Beethoven
to ringing phone or steady snore
beside me, and like Jove in

all his glory, I'm a lord
of metamorphosis,
however modest, having whored
myself for just one kiss

from Echo's tongue-tied sister.

FATHER SUTRA

Buddhists teach suffering comes
from fearing losing what one has,
so better have nothing,
but those who have kids,
fat chance they've got
unless one can lose
it all without fear.

BROTHERS AT BREAKFAST

People are like eggs, the younger says.
Some are scrambled, some are sunny-side-up.
From another room, with one sock on,
I want to add coddled or deviled,
but the older says first, *How about*
poached or hard-boiled? It's December,
month of black mornings. *Wouldn't you call*
Dad over-easy? the younger says.
Month of my birth and black afternoons.
Not really, the older replies.
I'd call him sunny-side-down.

CROSS COUNTRY PRACTICE

From Marathon Miltiades
sent good news to Athens
by means of fleet Pheidippides,
who ran, reported, died

as did a rival high school star
last week from too much heat.
It hasn't broken yet, yet here
you are, naked to the waist

no Greek chisel could improve
beside the slowing car,
your torso slick with leaking liquids.
But no lecture. Just a wave

and speeding up towards home in hope
I never see your grave.

ONE MORE THING A MATE MAKES FUN OF

might well be determination
to visit every single state and yet
without it one risks losing love
of America to fervent declarations
uninformed by intimate knowledge,
it being so easy, goodness knows,
to miss altogether remote North Dakota,
the center of our continent and still
a geographic wallflower, though how
anyone could smell the black dirt
of the Red River Valley and hear
a western meadowlark sparkling
through the prairie without wanting
a break from mountains or sea and wishing
to be Sioux is way beyond me.

ON THE ROCKS

You're not meeting my needs,
cracked red clay said to the sky
no rain had fallen from for months.
You leave me unsatisfied when I want
wells full, grass green, dust settled.

Tough, said the sky. You've had it easy.
Ask all the deserts; they find me generous.

PRESBYOPIA

Why does the inability of the eye
to focus sharply on what's nearby,
thanks to hardening of a crystalline lens,
come on now? Is it pure coincidence
that I finally see, in those closest to me,
the heart's small print more clearly?

BLURBS FOR THURSDAY

Elegantly alluring, strangely terrific, spell-bindingly
smashing sequel to Wednesday, impossible to put down,
engagingly funny, brilliantly humid, winds out of the west

simply stunning, the chance of rain unforgettable, wise,
haunting, full of passion and pathos, short-listed for best
day of the week beginning with T, destined to become

a mini-classic of mesmerizing magnificence, luminous
astonishment, searing intensity, its cicadas and crickets
sheer miracles of restraint, marvels of understatement,

humidly brilliant, the minutes right around noon particularly
well crafted, disturbing, remarkable, breathtaking, if you only
choose one day to get through this year make it this one,

vivid, compelling, poignantly realized cumulus clouds with
thrilling haze around the horizon, approaches the equinox
at the height of its powers, pure magic, don't miss it,

the hit of the season, sublime, magisterial, a tour de force
of late summer diminishment, a masterpiece of sluggish dawn
and earlier sunset, provocative, inspiring, a day

that showcases humdrum routine with exacting fidelity,
ambitious day, arresting day, gripping day, a day that dares
to risk nothing happening and pulls it off in total triumph,

sharp and sure, one of this year's most notable days,
provocative, no other like it, a pure pleasure,
life-changing, irresistible, a real must-live.

A WAY WITH WORDS

When you told me it wasn't the shell of a scallop
I brought you from the seashore, but the way I said
I brought you the shell of a scallop from the seashore
in a standard syntactic pattern, which by idealizing
clarity, transparency, and direct communication
operates complicitly with mass commodity culture
and subliminally rebroadcasts the social structure
while retreating into a realm of exalted subjectivity,

I felt like a steaming pile of fox scat
or someone who'd eaten a bushel of scallions
and forgotten to brush his teeth, and I wished
for a freshly sharpened scalpel to free me from scandal
without leaving a scar before too much more
of my scalp shines through a scarcity of hair
I share with scarecrows, who have never scanned
the fleshscape of your scapula or kissed it so much
you had nothing to say.

TAKE MY ADVICE

If I were you,
fleet of geese on the callusing pond,
I'd get along south right quick.

If I were you,
albino doe with three weeks to go
till rifle season's loud finale,
I'd keep my head low and roll it in some mud,
yes I would.

If I were one of you last five roses,
lipstick-colored on the bush outside,
and forecasts called for teens tonight,
I wouldn't delay whatever good-byes
I wanted to say.

As for you,
daylight gelded by another solstice,
I wouldn't sweat it. Your comeback's under way.

WINDSHAKE

Tree trunks strain in high west winds,
but not till chainsaws drop that timber
can you see the crack, a gap between growth rings
all that straining years ago caused.

We're not like that. Awful hours,
dreadful decades, they show outside, too,
in ways of walking, riven skin,
the wind-shook look of skittish eyes.

SACRIFICIAL

Take heart from the heifer Io became
and also the fountain née Arethusa.

Don't forget Daphne, later a laurel,
or reeds that used to look like Syrinx.

If bad things don't change, maybe you will
into red mangrove putting down roots

as thickets of stilts that suck up seawater
but send on salt to a few chosen leaves,

which filter you fresh, then yellow and drop
in tropical autumn back to warm ocean.

WAYS PEOPLE WAKE

Hungry, hung over, needing to pee,
regretting something done last night,
already dosed with morning morphine,
already late, on vacation, wholly unable
to get out of bed, eager, well rested,
ready to go, naked or clothed,
together, alone, smelly, stiff,
addicted to coffee, craving smoke,
with too much to do or not enough,
screaming in nightmare, about to come,
holding a gun, on the floor, on the ground,
with others to serve or be served by,
coughing, sneezing, prayer on the lips,
hissing obscenity, having drooled
or bled from the nose, sheets all wet,
dry in the throat from too much snoring,
sore in the jaws from too much grinding,
to rain unwanted or hoped for for months,
to garbage truck roar, still or moving
on a bus or a train, boat or plane,
to wake-up calls, alarm clocks, church chimes,
noisy animals, someone's voice saying gently
time to get up, or not so gently,
in the same place as always, in another
place unknown, in a room with a number,
as a guest, an inmate, a reconciled penitent,
in firm possession of a sense of purpose
or sunk in bereavement, back into blindness
having dreamed faces, back into deafness
having heard birds, chilly, sweaty,
beside the sea, covered in moonlight,
counting the hours till sleep comes again,
wishing one never had to go under.

WIND ADVISORY

Days like today
high profiles don't pay,
especially apparently
out on the interstate
where just like that
one good gust
can flip yo ass.

Stand up and be counted
some other day. For now,
dibs on the ditch,
gully, sunken road
between banked shoulders.
Keep low. Stay put.
Learn from the leaves.
No point in speeding
your own diaspora.

AMERICAN DREAM

What do I want? A harem?
Independent income? My name
breezing out of everybody's mouth?
No, just a small cell in a monastery
abandoned on a mountaintop above the sea,
old frescoes in the white-washed chapel
worn down to nothing but eyes,
enough oil for the icon lamps,
a stone well with cold water,
incense from an almond tree.

PATRIOTIC

Of course I am and pledge allegiance
To the ridgeline running between the summits
Of Lonesome and Sugarloaf, the saddle that joins them
Softer than a hogback, and to a piney pass up
And over to the Keswick side, where coastal plain
Floors the eye east all the way to the sea, leaving behind
My neck of woods, favorite outcrop,
Darling bank, sweetheart declivity
In this cherished country, whose body I love
And every day am dying for.

POLITICS

According to Aristotle,
it's the nature of nature
to do nothing uselessly
and the nature of desire
not to be satisfied,

so after the election,
narrowest nail-biter
or humiliating landslide,
why stew and fume?

If Aristotle's right
and reform can begin
only with desiring
nothing more, why not

join the jubilant
in desiring less,
especially for others?

JOGGER AT THE BLOODY ANGLE

She lopes upon the frenzy of the past
in blue running bra, red running shorts,
her ponytail keeping time in steady stride
like a metronome as yellow as new buttercups
along the road beside these earthworks.

Her shoes and music cost more dollars
than some who died here made in a year,
but dollars meant something different then,
and if she gives no thought to men
calf-deep in mud and purple puddles

from foggy dawn till long past midnight,
when the shot-up oak crashed down in rain
it's only fair. They gave the same to her.

A park's a park and green land rare
in so much progress, so many houses
standing now where Barlow crossed the Po.
Why should she know a thing about it?
Why should she care? She does her share

just running the route of that morning attack,
quitting the road and cantering the field
to disappear in dips and ripples of the ground
and teach the contours of its topography,

of dead space giving a little more life
to those who sheltered a few minutes there,
even better for her detachment.

SHERMAN, AFTER LOUISIANA

You mean to tell me that after all the pine
and Spanish moss wisping from bald cypress,
after the cattle egrets and common egrets
and snowy egrets rising from swamps and rivers
and bayous through spicy breezes soaked
with scented blossoms headier than anything
a lady in summer décolletage might dab
behind her ears or hidden knees or
along her low neckline to cool the space
around her as she leans over, laughing, after
the wine and accents like valleys
next to flat Ohio vowels, leans over
to touch a blue sleeve with just enough
showing to make the local tabasco
taste tepid and magnolia flowers
no match for her neck or shoulders
lighting the vacancy left by a family
waiting in another state, you mean to tell me
that even the scourge, the hun, the cruel barbarian,
even Satan himself could waste that landscape
without pools of remorse congealing inside him?

GENERAL POST OFFICE, DUBLIN

How can I promise
I'd differ from Thomas
and believe without touching
the prints of the nails,

when here I am feeling
the stone of each column
and sticking a finger
in bullet-made holes?

REFLECTIVE

from my observations Christ is little known by those who
consider themselves His friends
—JUAN DE LA CRUZ, *The Ascent of Mount Carmel*

tongue of light, what do you mean
by licking the wall that way,

and where do you come from, seeing as how
you clearly sheer off water mussed

by wind that never blows
in little rooms with windows closed

and water nowhere? are you one of those
organs of fire, hovering overhead,

or are you just a gesture that's rude,
stuck out through invisible lips

when a dog stops to drink some rising sun
from its metal bowlful out the window?

ARAMAIC IN SEDNAYA

In candlelight her tear-tracks outshine
icons all over the underground chapel,
even the one the faithful have come
so far to supplicate, the Virgin herself
painted by Luke, now on the wall
of a dark little grotto abstaining from sun,
where many believe that spending a night
will help them conceive, Christian and Muslim,
their shoes at the door whether they wear
headscarves or not, whether they make
signs of the cross again and again
before each image or dip some cotton
in bowls of oil and take it away
to someone sick who's left at home,
someone elsewhere who cannot see
tear-tracks shine in candlelight
or hear the old nun, the desert become
anything but desolate, begin to pray
in her savior's native tongue.

DESERT DESIDERATUM

Let loneliness be
esoteric ecstasy.

LOVE JUNK

A kiss onscreen would gross us out,
or so we said of all that love junk,
but the butterfly weed today's in bloom,
spindle-shaped seedpods having unfolded
to four big monarchs slowly pumping
four pairs of wings, orange on orange,
completely hooked on a single stalk,
as I'm now hooked, clean-cut addict,
on the very idea of kissing each canthus.

COASTAL ACOUSTICS

Not like a she-eagle,
silent in her flat-winged glide out over the bay,

broken by infrequent beats, until white feathers
of tail and head are all that show

against the spruce of a distant island.
And not like an osprey,

whose warning whistles sting the sky
once in a while when she soars off to fish

but stab repeatedly, riddling the blue,
when trespassers close on her nest.

And, no, not like a gull or fish-crow,
their coarse, gravelly grunts

much farther from it than a few of the calls
of a common loon, the quaver at night

or in thick fog her soprano flutter,
almost a chuckle, the sound you make.

LOWER WINDOW FOR VENTILATION

When a shaft of wind blasts the car,
cooling the bodies that bump one another
better than practiced partners,
and blows the hair of someone unseen
standing packed in next to me
up like a scarf around my cheeks,
a few wild strands tickling my ears
as I close my eyes to breathe in deeply
chamomile, lavender, rosemary, myrrh
from her shampoo, what more can earth do
for anyone traveling so far underground?

TO A PROSTITUTE ON FLEUR DE LIS STREET

If that's in fact what you truly are,
arm in arm with your partner here

in a narrow alley behind old factories,
derelict warehouses, she just a touch

younger than you, while a few yards away
hums the costly black car of whomever

you work for, whoever protects you.
Yes, a shade younger and probably she's

the thoughtless first choice of many who pass,
but a body that's firmer cannot be everything

in your line of work, and surely a few
discriminate acutely, those who appreciate

the refinements of experience. Or let's both hope so,
especially when it rains and business is slow,

your junior companion apparently untroubled
by aching feet or a throbbing hip,

when more than anything you have to hope something
to see yourself through the stale routines

with people whose needs and little demands
rarely examine the mysteries you've mastered.

PAIR OF ANKLETS, MUGHAL, INDIA, SEVENTEENTH CENTURY

Two brilliants, five diamonds, sixty-eight emeralds
from Colombia, and rubies galore. One thousand
twenty-two. But who did the counting?
And was it done in some museum or airless annex,
or while they decked two legs in action,
probably not dancing but maybe practicing
a particular page of the *Kama Sutra*, one of those ways
that would work the jewels up close to the eye
and keep them there, still, as long as it took
to number each gem by the flicker of torches
in a private pavilion out under the stars,
where quickness and closure could have no worth
for adepts who can dwell in the kiosk of a kiss.

EXCURSION INTO PHILOSOPHY

—Edward Hopper

Gimme the gamut, callipygian companion,
the full range of names your astonishing stern
cannot be named by. *Gluteal region?*
Coldly clinical. *Posterior? Possibly,*
but a little too priggish. *Derrière?*
We're American. *Ass?* Too animal.
Buttocks, backside, behind, buns?
What's with all the initial bilabials?
As for street mouth, where in *can,*
where in *keister,* where in *hiney,*
duff, tush, or *tail* resides the reverence,
the adequate awe, the sacredness sufficient
for someone mooned into speechless lunacy?
You see the problem: sickly signifiers
no one mistakes for sublime signifieds
when it comes to spooning after long days
of stubborn insistence that all things consist
of nothing but language. How can books,
which have helped so much, give no help here,
where darkest night makes way at first
for a blue-black of sloes and next for light
the bedroom window has boxed on floorboards?
Or maybe that's wrong, and maybe books do,
or this one does, open on the narrow bed
as you sleep still, facing the wall
in the sunlit altogether from your pelvis down,
a line dividing your two hemispheres,
a line between two cheeks of the book.

TEN TANKAS

High noon in autumn
And another ovulation
Of sun on its way
Down the blue tube of the sky,
Then out the west through red leaves.

Newly awakened,
With first hairs turning silver,
She never conceived
Any leaves could look so red
Or heat her with their color.

One has to wonder
What she feels beside the sea
When the sun makes waves
Break out at noon in hives of light
And scintillating goose bumps.

From bed she can see
Mars in the west setting red
And knows her yearning,
As heavy bombs drop elsewhere,
Looks to some like luxury.

Like something selfish,
A privilege of safety
Removed from places
Birds catch fire and bleed in flight,
A child's hand lies in rubble.

And perhaps it is
Blasphemy against the black
Canyons slashed through streets,
Factories, squares, hospitals
To dream of lovers and flush.

But if so, then why,
She asks herself next morning
As she bathes and stares
At the leaves out the window,
Why would the ancients have paired

Mars with Venus?
How could one sit on his lap,
Hooking an ankle
Around a calf, and slide herself
Down his belligerence?

She slips on her shoes,
Closes the door, and tiptoes
The border between
Vehemence and violence.
Oh, how can she understand

This secret coupling?
As though finding an answer
To such a question
Would one day enable her
To plant a seed in the sun.

SMALLER DOG

We can't all be
brightest in the sky

or the biggest guy
in outer space.

But I don't envy
anybody's place

or need to feel
I have no worth

because I'm far
from Orion's heel.

My yellow-white
double star

delivers its light
to nearby Earth

in eleven years flat,
which is pretty fast,

but my other boast
is Helen: she

loved me most
of all her hounds,

and you can't beat that.
So I, unsurpassed

in her esteem,
made no sounds

when secretly
they left for Troy.

He was the dream
igniting the dark

scarcity of joy.
How could I bark?

NEAR NORA

All domes lead to Rome,
the Pantheon's compression ring,
as all breasts bared beside this sea,
where Romans built on Phoenician leavings,
lead to thee.

COMMUNION OF SAINTS

In her soft mouth
a black bitch carries

sticks and balls,
a few small homicides,

fresh or putrefied,
and her favorite goody,

sun-dried cow dung,
whereas I have all

I can manage in mine
with this one tongue,

hurtful cause
of *ow* to some,

for one a source
of satisfied *oooo*,

under which I hide
the name *Bartholomew,*

though unstoried
throughout the gospels,

the patron saint
of average apostles.

TOOTHBRUSH

But I can't put toothbrushes in a poem. I really can't.
—SYLVIA PLATH, interview, October 30, 1962

Ah, but I can put a toothbrush
in her mouth, or would like to,
or even better yet would like to
be that toothbrush in her mouth,

my purple plastic shaft enclosed
in her precious fist, my bristling head
awash in foam as I swirl sweet suds
flavored with cinnamon or clove or mint

over the molars, canines, incisors
I do not judge for whiteness or wish
straighter or less crowded as I sweep
the bristles themselves, firm and fresh,

over their surfaces, inside and outside,
upper and lower, each chip or crack
or cavity dear to me as history
of her sweet tooth for this or that,

her nighttime grindings, daylight gnashings
without which how could she ever be
worth the trouble or the daily care
first thing at morning when her mouth

tastes bad to her, if not to me,
and last thing at night before she
folds into bed and whatever's awaiting
her there? But only after

I've lightly stroked the tender gums
and scrubbed the savory tongue
against disease, against bacteria,
against having to say anything but *Ah.*

IF THE *KAMA SUTRA* WERE
OUR ONLY BOOK

If the *Kama Sutra* were our only book,
what could one say
of a single white deer in a field at sunset,
lone albino amidst brown siblings?

That it bites the eye like *coral and jewel*
or *broken cloud* between the breasts?

That it rubs the mind or presses or churns,
as the mind takes it in like a *pair of tongs,*
blow of a boar, sporting of a sparrow?

And what of the sounds, pigeon gurgle,
parrot squawk, serpent hiss,
that won't stay down once attention's aroused

by a sight that scratches memory's skin,
pervious, incisable, with *tiger's nail,*
peacock's foot, leaf of blue lotus?

UNSPOKEN AGREEMENT

When I say I as in I
believe in the forgiveness of sins
or would like a cup of the soup du jour, please,

I know you know it's just a sobriquet
for what lights up in rainbow ways
my ventral putamen and prefrontal cortex

under positron emission tomography,
magnetoencephalography, functional resonance imaging
without your having to say so.

And when you say I as in I, meaning you,
pledge allegiance to the flag or swear to tell the whole truth
or wish you'd touch me this way there now,

you know I know what's cooking in your thalamus
as clearly as if you'd said my limbic system
sure hums high and both my sets of cortices,

motor and somatosensory,
are ready to roll so let me let
my larynx loose, though not in so many words.

BEAT THIS, NARCISSUS

Mirror, mirror, above the sink
of a bathroom in a swank hotel,
what the hell do you really think
she sees in me?

Take a gander, naked man,
at your verso in a full-length glass
on the background door
as you bend to splash

and consider the sight,
run-of-the-mill as it may well be,
from her point of view
when upright, behind you.

THAT DESIRE IS A WISH TO ENGAGE IN SEXUAL ACTIVITY AND OF ITS TRIGGERING BY THOUGHTS OR VERBAL AND VISUAL CUES

—The Merck Manual

Ooh-la-la, somewhere the coconuts are rolling
down a steep beach after each wave
has nudged them up the cinnamon sand
and receded. Somewhere. You bet.

And somewhere flamingos nap on one leg
in the shade of date palms, looking good,
as egrets nab small fish in shallows
and sunset matches a slice of papaya.

In such a place the pile of night
feels smooth and dense as that of velvet.
In such a place breeze from the sea
tousles bamboo and warms like rum.

No arctic air mass there. No glass that sweats
with condensation, all windows cataracts,
their sashes water-logged, and on one sill,
facing south with other bric-a-brac,

a miniature cast in dusty plaster,
the sandaled foot of broken Venus
toughing it out with no wool sock
or fur-lined boot. Attagirl.

BESIDE THE POINT

The sky has never won a prize.
The clouds have no careers.
The rainbow doesn't say *my work*,
thank goodness.

The rock in the creek's not so productive.
The mud on the bank's not too pragmatic.
There's nothing useful in the noise
the wind makes in the leaves.

Buck up now, my fellow superfluity,
and let's both be of that worthless ilk,
self-indulgent as shooting stars,
self-absorbed as sunsets.

Who cares if we're inconsequential?
At least we can revel, two good-for-nothings,
in our irrelevance; at least come and make
no difference with me.

TASTE THE FRESH JUICE OF
THE POMEGRANATES

I shall see you in your heat,
and you will see me in your heat,
and I shall see myself in you in your heat,
and you will see yourself in me in your heat,
that I may resemble you in your heat,
and you resemble me in your heat,
and my heat be your heat,
and your heat be my heat,
wherefore I shall be you in your heat,
and you will be me in your heat,
because your very heat will be my heat,
and we shall see each other in your heat.

À GRANDE VITESSE

Beside the tracks, Paris to Bordeaux,
leafless trees keep breaking out
in balls of mistletoe

whose parasitic pompoms
clot the crotches of the branches
with promises of kisses.

Le gui they call it here,
where Roman farmers planted vines
and this or that exceptional year

still tastes of Caesar.
But why buy wine
one could die before drinking

at full maturity, a decade or so
off in the future? Farsighted sybarites
presumably know

just the right ratio
of pleasure to providence;
yet where in these vineyards, their chateaux

flashing past, where in quick villages,
each with its own, Decembery cold,
unheated churchful of ether-sweet incense,

do you find one of those?

PARKINSON'S CLINIC, CEZANNE
ON THE WALL

Bully for the bottle
that bellies to the right
and for the tumult in blue drapes;
bully for the tabletop and tall decanter,
for apples, glass, and rebellious surface.

Bully for you
who have rebuilt what seeing means
with canvas and a little oil
and with your work have far surpassed
habits of bland cognition.

Please accept these thanks
for epistemic mussings up
to keep all things in some perspective

without which many, or some, or a few
would feel themselves the hopeless drones
of common sense and surely wilt,

but please excuse the ones
experiment in stable lines
of sight upset can never save,
their last capacities to process
gone or rusting through

and stripped of means
to recognize this simple syntax
for what it is, what is clear

now lost on them
in their condition every day

makes avant-garde.

MISSIONARY POSITION

Glaciers are melting and tumors on testicles
or lump-breeding breasts keep stealing our favorites,

but, frost-nicked morning glory, if you take requests
for that indigo gramophone you aim at the sun,

hold off on the one about the problem of pain
and please play instead another theodicy,

one that explains why powers that be
allow us our ecstasies when elegy rules.

BUTT-NAKED OLD MEN

Not a pretty picture
in the public pool locker room,
but now, now, no need to get all
ubi sunt or *carpe diem* about it.

So once upon a time that slackened anatomy
embodied Adonis in somebody's eyes,
the incarnation of a trembling crush
exquisitely fulfilled or forever unrequited,

and now stands crushed itself,
skin discolored, whatever the color,
and overgrown with growths enough
to keep dermatologists dancing.

As for that distinguishing feature
among these noontime nudists, the one that meant
frustration to some, triumph to others,
and to a few a bothersome distraction,

it looks unlikely its status will be
ever elevated to most preferred.

But stick that pity in some other ear;

once upon a time can only deject
those who live so far beyond it,

unlike a new mother just diagnosed
and never to bare her fatal breasts,
lucky to last and wither at last,

over on the ladies' side.

THE STORY OF MY LIFE

light hair
dark hair
light hair

OLD DOGS

No more rambles on the rocky shore
with chances to chase a black-backed gull,
munch on clam shells, pee in fireweed.

No more jaunts to the top of the mountain
for scary bear scat or discarded deer offal
to roll and wallow in.

And weirdest of all, no more tail-chasing,
mouth-watering fawns and savory squirrels
way too fast to put out after.

Now a blind eye, deaf ear,
now the stiff back and bad hips,
now with their teeth slowly dropping out
the one desire left

to lick and sniff (hey, you smell good)
and lie in the sun, usually parallel,
sometimes perpendicular, but always,
if possible, touching each other

as though in heaven or just about to be.

TO FUTURE PEOPLE

This ritual palette of King Narmer,
carved of slate and used for cosmetics,
records his conquest of Lower Egypt
five thousand years before the ash tree drops
pollen pods yet one more time.

Another spring. In five thousand more
do trees still bloom and you still sneeze?
Are forests gone or better than ever?

Thanks to an implant or genetic procedure
or maybe a pill or potent nasal spray,
is aging as quaint as worshipping wind gods
and love archaic as infant sacrifice?

And what about reverence, yours for us,
our ancient wisdom, or do you
think us clods, poorly recording
basic features we took for granted,

a loaf of white cloud, a spall of sunlight
in a certain eye, which rarely, if ever,
thought itself something, let alone
something someday lost to you?

CLASPED

Between the end and when
it's gone forever cold,
a hand can hold its heat
for many minutes,

and one who holds that hand
can feel as warmed by it
as when the heat felt endless
for many minutes.

HOME ON LEAVE

Where I come from the Ice Age left
  so many stones, glacial spare change,

the ground's no good for growing much
  except grass that goes for feed or hay,

and, even then, only once some farmer
  cleared the stones into low gray walls

marking the bounds of rectangle fields
  long since lost in second-growth woods.

What a lot of work for all those backs
  whose sturdy spines are very likely

still intact in these country graves.
  Come nightfall, it's time to turn

from the freshest one, from understatement
  of name and date, and leave the cemetery

for woods that surround it, stumbling there
  on an old stone wall that one can follow

deeper into leafy darkness or just admire
  for the labor of such durable vertebrae.

GRAPE HYACINTH

I'm glad the grass is overgrown
and glad the mower's in the shop,
with oil to change and blade to hone,
so I don't have to cut this crop
of showy spikes, the purplish blue
that puts the slipshod lawn to shame.
I know we don't look well-to-do;
I know our yard just isn't the same
as other members of its class,
neatly trimmed and closely shorn.
But let them bloom in the uncut grass
and prettify a time to mourn.

TRIMMED WITH CREPE

It will be as well to consider in succession
the different degrees of mourning.
—*Collier's Cyclopedia*, 1901

Nature has no taste,
Wren and bluebird oblivious
To the ban on gold and silver,

To ornament of any kind
For at least nine months
In the first deep year.

It shouldn't have occurred
With pear trees in full bloom.
Her name was my first word,

Her younger sister said,
And still the dense black coal
Of sudden only-childhood

Takes the high polish
Of jet, the lone exception
Permissible for jewelry.

MOTHER'S DAY CARD

Looked up *sastruga* and thought of you
snowed in in Maine in a house by the bay
white with sea smoke in cold below zero

and every walk through shoveled tunnels
with fewer groceries or the reluctant dog,
for mail without letters or the daily paper

after a sunset that comes before four
or under thick stars or green northern lights
a widow's walk.

No need to watch
for particular ships out on the water;
no need to stay in the house you called his,

and yet you do, learning to snowshoe
through the deep fields grooved with sastrugi
as flimsy sun strengthens, last drifts dissolve,

and black flies come on for that spindly spring,
not all one could wish for but accepted just the same,
even, at seventy, something to welcome

like the baby that took you too young by surprise.

TO ALL THE DREAMS I HAVE FORGOTTEN

Tens of thousands you must be by now
after fifty years of one-night stands,
a new Scheherazade each sleep and she,
like all her sorority, ready to wow
the graveyard shift that ends at dawn
the same as the quickest catnap.

Never mind what you might have meant
by an eagle's head on a cumulus cloud
or a father, dead, swimming through orange juice;
thanks for coming and good for you
for getting away, unremembered, unread,
with the inside stories of a loudmouth life.

WORLD EVENTS

Why am I,
Who cannot fly
Or sing a song

And have no mask
As black as his,
Allowed to see

A cardinal killed,
His feathered hood
So red in the road?

AFTER THE BOMBINGS

After the bombings it's hard to hear
any seduction in the sound of sirens
harrowing streets sapped of traffic,

as though this weekday, fed up with its workload,
had suddenly quit to become a sabbath.

Even an upstart day of rest
must have its share of usual stabbings,
smaller states of private emergency,
the overdose here, attempted rape there,
which some of the sirens must be announcing,

or is the worst not nearly over
and this the music of final uncovering
when cruciform you, church, tree, or friend,
will fold me in your transept arms?